Unit Five: Peer Relationships

Have a
Good Day

What is something kind that a friend has done for you? How did that make you feel?

In this story, the kids help Z learn that there are many ways to be kind and help someone else have a good day. Showing kindness and caring toward others can make them feel special, and can make you feel good too.

As you listen to the story, pay attention to the kind things that Z and the kids do for one another.

It was a beautiful day at the tree house and Z couldn't wait to see the kids. Z was in a really happy mood and was having a very good day.

"Hi, Jordan! Hi, Mia!" Z called out the window.

"Hi, Z!" answered the kids. "Do you want to play today? We brought some paper so we could all paint pictures together!"

"Come on up!" exclaimed Z.

As the kids climbed the ladder to the tree house, Z turned around and saw the table. It was a big mess! That was going to make it hard for everyone to paint. Z quickly gathered up the scattered crayons and markers and put them into a box. Then Z pulled out the paints and brushes and set them on the table.

When the kids came into the tree house, they were very surprised to see the table all cleaned and organized.

"Wow, Z!" said Jordan. "Thank you for getting everything ready for us to paint!"

"You must really like to do kind things for people!" added Mia.

While they were painting, Z remembered that the kids both liked elephants, so Z painted a purple elephant for Jordan and a red elephant for Mia. That made both the kids smile.

"Thank you, Z!" said Mia happily. "It makes me feel special that you made this for me!"

Seeing Jordan and Mia so happy made Z feel very good inside.

"You sure seem very happy today, Z," said Jordan.

"I do feel happy!" answered Z, "But I'm not really sure why."

"I think it's because you are having a good day," said Mia, "And you have been helping us to have a good day too! When you do kind things for people, it makes everyone feel good."

"I want to do that!" exclaimed Z. "What else could I do?"

"Well," explained Jordan, "You can help someone have a good day by saying kind things to them, or helping them, or doing something nice for them. Just like all the things that you have been doing today, Z!"

When the kids finished their pictures, they hung them up to dry. Mia noticed that Z couldn't reach, so she offered to hang Z's pictures. Z felt warm inside and gave Mia a big hug. "Thanks, Mia!"

Z wanted everyone to keep having a good day, so Z helped the kids put away the paints and then shared some muffins with them. After that, Z invited Jordan and Mia to play ball.

Z grinned happily. "I'm so glad that I helped my friends have a good day, and they helped me have a good day too!"

Z says,
"Whenever we're together my friends help me discover how children on earth get along with each other!"

Z wants all of you to remember that being kind to one another can help everyone have a good day.

Connecting to the Classroom

➤ **Everyday Moment:** Focus on children's prosocial behavior.

- ▸ Point out children's prosocial actions (e.g., *That was really nice sharing!*).

- ▸ Highlight children's prosocial disposition (e.g., *You are really someone who likes to help others!*).

- ▸ Call attention to the positive consequences of prosocial actions (e.g., *When you gave Tina a turn on the swing, it made her really happy*).

- ▸ Invite the other child to share their feelings (e.g., *Jason, I noticed that Lilia shared her stickers with you. How did that made you feel?*).

➤ **Discussions and Activities**

- ▸ Discuss what gratitude means.

- ▸ Have children describe how they feel when they do kind things for others and why they feel that way.

- ▸ Have children practice giving compliments to their buddies, and showing gratitude when receiving a compliment.

- ▸ Have children create and exchange a memento (e.g., *bracelets or cards*) with their buddies.

Including Everyone

How do you feel when someone invites you to play with them?

In this story, the kids help Z learn that it is kind to include others when you play. There are a lot of ways you can make sure that everyone feels included.

As you listen to the story, pay attention to how Z and the kids figure out ways to include others in a game.

One sunny afternoon, Z, Kayla and Mia were playing tic-tac-toe in the tree house. They had been playing the same game for a long time and Z was starting to feel wiggly! Z wiggled and squirmed and fidgeted.

"Can we play something else now?" asked Z.

Mia got a big box from the table.

"We just got this new game," she said. "It's called Rumble Jumble and it's really fun! Do you want to play this now?"

Z looked at the game board. "I don't know how to play Rumble Jumble," said Z sadly. "I guess I'll go find something else to do."

"We want you to be able to play too," said Mia. "If you want, Kayla and I can play first and you can watch us and learn how to play. Then we can all play together."

The kids spread out the colorful game pieces and started playing Rumble Jumble. Z watched and tried hard to remember the rules.

After a little while, Jeremy and Kim arrived at the tree house.

"Hey, is that Rumble Jumble?" Jeremy asked excitedly. "I love that game!"

"Me too!" said Kim. "Can we play with you?"

Z looked around at the pieces on the table.

"There aren't enough pieces for everyone to play. There's only room for me and one more person."

Z pointed at Kim. "So you can play, Kim, but Jeremy can't."

"I guess I'll just play something else by myself," said Jeremy sadly.

Whoops-Z!

Z didn't know that there can be lots of ways to make sure that everyone feels included.

What would you tell Z to do?

"Z," said Mia. "It would be really nice if we could find a way to include Jeremy too."

Kayla nodded. "Being left out doesn't feel very good," she said. "And playing is much more fun when we include everyone!"

"I'm sorry, Jeremy," said Z. "I didn't mean to leave you out. Will you play with us too?"

"Thanks, Z," said Jeremy. "But there are still only enough pieces for one more person to play. I guess I still won't be able to play."

"No way!" said Z. "I know we can find a way to include everyone!"

"Maybe one of us can play with a partner," suggested Mia. "That's one way that we all can play together."

Z bounced up and down excitedly. "Would someone be my partner? I still have a lot to learn about playing Rumble Jumble!"

Mia volunteered to be Z's partner, so they passed out the pieces and started the game again.

"Thanks for making room for me to play," said Jeremy. "This is a lot of fun!"

Z and all of the kids had a great time playing Rumble Jumble together all afternoon. It really was much more fun to include everyone!

Z says,
"Whenever we're together my friends help me discover how children on earth get along with each other!"

Z wants you to remember that it feels really good to be included. You can figure out lots of way to make room for everyone and to make sure that everyone feels included.

Connecting to the Classroom

- **Everyday Moment:** Promote and reinforce welcoming and inclusive play.

  - Point out how good it makes others feel to be included.

  - Set clear classroom expectations about exclusion, and do not allow exclusion based on gender or any other social category.

- **Discussions and Activities**

  - Discuss how it feels to be left out of something others are doing.

  - Discuss what it means to include others, and have children think of ways to invite someone to join them.

  - Discuss when it may be okay to say "no" to someone who wants to play with you (e.g., *when you want to play alone, when there isn't enough room*) and how to do so kindly.

  - Play "reverse musical chairs" where children are invited into the circle by a classmate each time the music stops until everyone has been included. Discuss how it feels to be included and how it feels to have to wait to be included.

Staying
Friends

An *accident* is something that someone doesn't do on purpose. Have you ever done something by accident that made someone else upset or hurt their feelings? What happened? What did you do to make things better?

In this story, Z and the kids accidentally hurt one another's feelings. The kids help Z learn that even when that happens, you can still figure out how to make things better and stay friends.

As you listen to the story, pay attention for times when Z and the kids feel hurt by something that someone else has done, and what they do so that they are able to stay friends.

One morning, Z woke up very, very early because there was a bird chirping loudly in the tree house window. Z yawned and stretched.

"Good morning, Z!" said Jordan, as he came through the door. "I brought you some muffins that I helped my big sister make this morning."

Z picked a warm muffin from the basket and took a big bite. It was so yummy!

"Do you want to draw with me, Z?" asked Jordan.

With a tummy full of muffins, Z was feeling very sleepy. "Maybe later," said Z, with a yawn. "I woke up early and I'm tired."

Jordan was working on his picture when Annie arrived at the tree house.

"Guess what?" said Annie. "Yesterday my brother showed me how to make a birdhouse! Do you want to help me gather some twigs and sticks so we can make one?"

"That sounds like fun! Z, do you want to come too?"

But Z was fast asleep!

"Z was really tired," Jordan explained. "I guess we'll just go by ourselves and let Z rest."

Later in the morning, Z woke up from a nice long nap.

"What are you doing?" Z asked the kids.

"We're building a birdhouse," answered Annie excitedly. "It's almost finished—do you want to see it?"

Z did not want to see the birdhouse. Z felt hurt and angry that the kids built it without Z.

"I don't want to see your birdhouse. Birdhouses are silly," grumbled Z. "I'm just going to play by myself."

Annie and Jordan looked sad. "Don't you want to play with us, Z?"

"No, I don't want to play," answered Z. "I didn't get to help make the birdhouse, so we're not friends anymore."

Whoops-Z!

Z's feelings are hurt, and now Z thinks they can't play together or be friends anymore.

What would you tell Z to remember?

"Z, you're right," said Jordan kindly. "We did have a part in what happened—we thought you wanted to sleep so we didn't wait for you to make the birdhouse."

Z sighed. "I'm glad you told me what happened. I know you didn't leave me out on purpose, but I still wish I could have helped."

"We're sorry you're sad," said Annie "We didn't mean to hurt your feelings. But we can still be friends!"

Z was worried. "But I wasn't nice to you—I said that birdhouses were silly."

"Sometimes friends make mistakes and hurt each other's feelings," the kids explained. "But if we forgive each other and let go of our sad and mad feelings, we can make things better."

Z already felt a little better. "I didn't mean to hurt your feelings when I said that we weren't friends anymore. I won't say that again, even if I'm mad."

The kids thought about how to fix what happened and make things better with Z.

"I know!" Annie said. "There's a way that you can still help! Can you use your long arms to hang the birdhouse outside?"

Z carefully hung the birdhouse in the tree. The beautiful bird that Z had seen that morning flew right inside and began to sing a cheerful song. Z and the kids smiled at one another and were glad that they were still friends.

Z says,
"Whenever we're together my friends help me discover how children on earth get along with each other!"

Z wants all of you to remember that when you don't get along, you can still figure out how to make things better and stay friends.

Connecting to the Classroom

➢ **Everyday Moment:** Focus on empathic responses to children's strong emotions—even negative ones.

 ▸ Provide caring support to children when they are experiencing strong or overwhelming emotions.

 ▸ Make it clear that it is okay to feel angry or upset or hurt, but it is not okay to act upon these feelings in unkind ways.

 ▸ Support children in calming down and exercising self-control in order to be able to apologize or forgive.

➢ **Discussions and Activities**

 ▸ Discuss what it means to forgive someone, and why it is important to be a fast forgiver.

 ▸ Discuss what to do when you have hurt someone, even if it was an accident.

 ▸ Introduce an "Apology in Action":

  ▪ *Say your part* – *stay calm and explain what happened*

  ▪ *Speak from the heart* – *say something kind to let the other person know that you care about what happened*

  ▪ *Fix what has been broken apart* – *find a way to make things better*

 ▸ Have buddies role play a conflict scenario and demonstrate an "Apology in Action".

Remembering Friends

What is something special that you remember about this school year?

In this story, Z and the kids think back on the time they have spent with one another and all of the memories that they have together.

As you listen to the story, pay attention to how the kids and Z feel as they remember their time together, and listen for what they hope will happen in the future.

One afternoon, Z, Kenny, Gabriel, and Kayla were straightening up the tree house after a busy day of playing. Suddenly, Z exclaimed, "Look, everyone! Look what I found!"

Z had discovered a big box with a stack of old drawings inside. The kids gathered around Z and everyone began looking through the pictures.

"That's me!" said Z, holding out a drawing of when Z first arrived on earth.

"I made that drawing!" said Kayla. "I remember going outside and finding you and your rocket ship behind the bushes. I was so excited to meet you, but also a little bit nervous."

"I used to feel really shy too," said Z softly. "I didn't know anything about kids."

Gabriel gave Z's hand a squeeze. "But then we played together and found out what we had in common, right? Now we know a lot about each other!"

Z pulled another drawing out of the box. "Now I remember something that we did not have in common," said Z, pointing to the picture of a caterpillar. "We did not all like bugs!"

The kids laughed. "You're right, Z! We all wanted to do different things with the caterpillar that you found in the tree house. We really had to figure that out together!"

"We took care of that caterpillar for a long time," said Kenny. "Do you remember how much fun it was when it changed into a butterfly and we let it fly away?"

Everyone nodded and smiled as they thought about that day.

Then Z held up another drawing and looked a little sad. "The day that some of the kids made a birdhouse wasn't a very fun day," said Z. "That was the day that we hurt each other's feelings. I didn't think that we could still be friends."

"Don't be sad, Z," said Gabriel. "Sometimes it's hard to get along. But we have always worked it out and we're all still friends."

Z smiled. "You're right—everyone has helped me learn so much about how children on earth get along with each other."

Z kept digging through some more drawings. "What's this one?" Z asked in a puzzled voice.

Kenny started giggling. "That's a drawing I made of you one day when you had the ziggles! I will always remember the way that you dance when you feel ziggly!"

Z wiggled and twirled around. "Do you mean like this?"

"Yes!" answered the kids. "Ziggly just like that!"

"And here's how we would help you calm down when you got too ziggly," said Kayla. "It's a picture of the bubble machine!"

"Oh, I remember the bubble machine!" said Z. "We used to lay in the grass and watch the bubbles and talk and laugh for hours! That was one of my favorite things to do with my friends!"

Z and the kids spread the rest of the drawings out on the table.

"We sure had a lot of good times together," said Gabriel. "I think I'm going to remember all of my friends at the tree house even when I'm a big kid."

Z thought about all the kids from the tree house and the time they had spent together. Z smiled and felt warm inside, and Z hoped that they would all be friends for a very, very long time.

Z says,
"Whenever we're together my friends help me discover how children on earth get along with each other!"

Z wants all of you to remember the time that you have spent with your classmates and the ways that you have grown and learned and changed together this year.

Connecting to the Classroom

➢ **Everyday Moment:** Take time to share a meaningful reflection with each child in your classroom.

 ▸ Share a specific message about how you have seen them grow.

 ▸ Tell children about something you will remember about them.

 ▸ Point out ways in which they have made a positive impact on you, their classmates, or the classroom community.

➢ **Discussions and Activities**

 ▸ Have children reflect on how they felt at the beginning of the school year and what it was like to meet new classmates.

 ▸ Discuss with children how their feelings have stayed the same or changed since the beginning of the year and why.

 ▸ Ask children to share some of their favorite memories from the school year.

 ▸ Have children make a banner together that highlights memories from the school year.